Relaying the Word
A 16-Week Trek through the Bible with Friends

TINA: It was a true inspiration to listen to the individual experiences and how they related to the verse we were reading. When God blesses participants and they share, you also receive a blessing.

SHANNON: What a blessing! We looked forward to Monday night and our discussions with our group. This Bible study made our faith stronger, and I believe that my husband and I have grown as a couple because of it.

JODI: It's a lifestyle change in reading the Bible that doesn't quit when the study is over!

**Relaying the Word:
A 16-Week Trek through the Bible with Friends**
Beyr Reyes
Copyright @ 2016 ShadeTree Publishing, LLC
Print ISBN: 978-1-937331-88-7
e-Book ISBN: 978-1-937331-89-4

All rights reserved. This book is protected by copyright. No part of this book may be reproduced or transmitted in any form or by any means, electronic or mechanical, including photocopying, recording, or by any information storage and retrieval system, without permission in writing from the publisher.

The purpose of this book is to educate and enlighten. This book is sold with the understanding that the author and publisher are not engaged in rendering counseling, albeit it professional or lay, to the reader or anyone else. The author and publisher shall have neither liability nor responsibility to any person or entity with respect to any loss or damage caused, or alleged to have been caused, directly or indirectly, by the information contained in this book.

Visit our Web site at www.ShadeTreePublishing.com.

About Relaying the Word

Relaying the Word is an answer to many holes in people's lives.. 1

The purpose of Relaying the Word is to learn the Word of God together so that we can run our race to win. 3

Drafting a team for Relaying the Word is easy. 5

The 16-week game plan of Relaying the Word is intuitive and straightforward... 9

Relaying the Word is a lifetime race. 71

Appendix: Extra Material to Help with the Readings 73

Review Request 103

About the Author.. 105

Other Books by Beyr Reyes 106

Relaying the Word is an answer to many holes in people's lives.

People are searching for something because they feel a void in their lives, and because they do not fully understand what exactly is missing, many try to fill the absence they feel with drugs, alcohol, work, exercise, or sex. They are treating the symptoms and bringing about temporary fixes.

The biggest hole in people's life is the place where God should be—and this is even true for many Christians. Other holes include having real relationships and knowing our true purpose on earth. *Relaying the Word* addresses these voids and more. It fosters a safe place where people can build relationships with others and with the Word.

Relaying the Word is an authentic Bible study that is akin to spiritual Crossfit. Together we will build up and encourage the Body of Christ through fellowship and the Word.

Relaying the Word

The purpose of Relaying the Word is to learn the Word of God together so that we can run our race to win.

Relaying the Word is a nondenominational curriculum. No personal agendas. No doctrine. Just the Word.

Yes, the purpose of *Relaying the Word* is to build relationships with others and with the Word. However, the additional objectives go much deeper than that. Together, the participants will:

- Learn the Word of God and how to apply it to their everyday life, especially in a volatile society.
- Decide what they stand for, instead of just what they are against—and be able to defend the reasons why for each case.
- Discover what the Word says about them specifically, including their purpose in life.
- Begin to hear the Lord speaking to them, especially if they have never heard His voice before.
- Develop relationships that are real and enduring.
- Ask tough questions without judgment.
- Know Jesus, either for the first time or more intimately.

Although the study can be done alone, it is much more powerful with a group that shares testimonies, accountability, and encouragement. *Relaying the Word* is a time to plug in to socialness instead of social media, and it fosters true fellowship instead of online fakeness. It works for all ages, levels of faith, and Christian denominations, and it works best when there is a combination of all of these together.

The culture of *Relaying the Word* does not end when the study ends. It is meant to be passed like a runner's baton, and they should be followed up on by plugging in to a ministry in a local church, continuing to read the Word, and keeping and strengthening new connections. Perhaps participants will even consider leading another study by using this manual. Above all, though, we must run our race to win and not forget that we are all running together—maybe not all in the same lane, but definitely all on the same team.

God intends for His people to finish strong. It is my desire that when you get to the end of your race, you will hear Him say, "Well done, My good and faithful servant," and I pray that *Relaying the Word* has helped you somewhere along the way.

Drafting a team for Relaying the Word is easy.

Announce the Study and Gather Interest

The very first step in starting a *Relaying the Word* series is to decide when to begin. Allow for sixteen weeks for the entire series, and take into account all holidays and vacation times, as well as the potential for inclement weather. See the *Schedule of Reading* section in the appendix for a week-by-week plan.

The next step is to recruit participants. Social media is powerful for spreading the word. Also, make an announcement in your own church (after receiving a green light from your pastor) and have friends do the same. Your local newspaper can help, too. Check out their social media, website, and print guidelines.

Handle Excuses

Following are the most commonly encountered excuses. The key to debunking each excuse or doubt is to provide an alternative way to overcome it and a bit of encouragement to do so.

Excuse: I don't have time to read.
Excuse: I don't like to read.
Excuse: I can't read fast or well.

Relaying the Word

Reply: Listen to an audio version of the Bible while at work, in the car, on the train, etc.

Excuse: I've tried to read the Bible before and I just don't understand it.
Reply: Try a different version of the Bible. (Offer the *Information about Bible Versions* section in the appendix for help in deciding which version to use.)

Excuse: I only read a certain version of the Bible.
Reply: There is no "correct" Bible version to use for this Bible study. In fact, we welcome all the versions, because this leads to better and more interesting discussions and different perspectives. (Offer the *Information about Bible Versions* section in the appendix for help in knowing what each Bible version is like.)

Excuse: I've already read the Bible several times.
Reply: Try listening instead, or try a different version. New ways of input can unlock hidden verses and open your mind to new meanings. Also, the Word of God is a living thing, which God will use to speak different messages to you in different seasons of your life. Furthermore, if you have read the Bible several times, then you would be a great addition to the discussion when complicated questions arise.

Excuse: Reading the Bible over sixteen weeks is too fast to absorb anything.
Reply: The goal of this study is not to catch everything, but to listen to what the Lord highlights for you. The discussions of the reading will fill in many gaps and help you to remember and understand things you read, but thought you missed.

Excuse: I can't afford to make the meetings.
Response: Try attending via Skype, Google hangout, etc. Meetings can be recorded and uploaded to a private group site.

Establish the Who, When, and Where

Once you start promoting an upcoming *Relaying the Word* study, start collecting the names and contact information of any interested folks—even if they have not decided for certain yet. An easy thing to do is to create a closed group on Facebook or some other common social media site and start adding members who have signed up or who are still deciding. This group page will be a great place to make announcements during the sixteen-week study. (Just be sure to remove anyone who does not end up attending.)

After assessing the number of attendants, decide on a location that can house and be the most convenient for the group. Also, decide on the best day of the week and time for everyone to attend.

Schedule the informational meeting (Week 1), at which time the details of the remaining fifteen weeks of the study will be explained.

Relaying the Word

The 16-week game plan of Relaying the Word is intuitive and straightforward.

Having a game plan removes the stress of knowing what to do. This simple and easy-to-follow participant guide lays out step-by-step how to conduct the sixteen-week *Relaying the Word* study.

Each week of this Bible study is clearly outlined. A typical meeting consists of the following:

1. Pre-meeting Food and Fellowship
When establishing the schedule for the meetings, be sure to formally schedule some time directly before each meeting as "food and fellowship time." An hour of time is recommended, but thirty minutes will suffice if time is an issue.

For best results, start the carry-in dinner at 6:00 p.m. and the meeting at 7:00 p.m. People can arrive and eat anytime during the fellowship time. This allows them to enter a relaxed atmosphere instead of feeling like they are racing against the clock to arrive as soon as they can without creating distractions or interruptions.

Because of hectic schedules, a group may be tempted to forego a time to eat and fellowship before the meetings. It is *strongly* advised, however, that the importance of this time of breaking bread together is not overlooked!

During the fellowship time, people are able to unwind from the day's events and start getting in the mood to talk so they won't be clammed up during the discussions. It is also a time to share testimonies and personal stories from the previous week, while sparing later discussion of unrelated personal stories. Fellowship time builds relationship and trust. People will open up more during the discussions if safety has already been established. Without the fellowship time together, it is likely that the discussion at the meetings will be thin and shallow.

Because it can be burdensome for a single individual to provide all of the food for a meal, it is advised that a theme be chosen for each meeting, and everyone bring a little something that would be enough to feed them or their family in attendance plus a couple more. Popular food themes include Mexican, Asian, other ethnic choices, pasta, cookout, finger foods and appetizers, pizza, sandwiches, potluck, soups and salads, etc. It is also best that everyone be in charge of bringing their own drink and that specific people be designated for dessert(s). A signup sheet is the best way to keep everyone aware of the weekly food themes. Also, be sure to check the reading schedule or the calendar for Jewish holidays with special foods that could be incorporated in the weekly meal. See the *Feasts and Special Holidays* section in the appendix for more information.

2. Opening Prayer

It is important to open each meeting with a word of prayer. For best results, designate a person to lead the prayer in advance. This can be done by asking someone publicly or privately during the fellowship time. If no one volunteers, then the meeting leader or house host should lead the prayer.

Following are some things to pray for, in addition to any specific prayer requests or praise reports from the participants.

- Thank God for His Word.
- Ask God to open hearts, ears, and minds to receive His Word.
- Ask God to protect the group from the enemy and any plans he has for confusion, condemnation, or judgment.
- Ask the Holy Spirit to help the group to be doers of the Word and not just readers.
- Ask God for an environment of encouragement.
- Ask for peace, joy, and love to saturate the discussion.
- Ask the Holy Spirit to move among the group and have His way.
- Ask for hidden revelations to be revealed.

3. Accountability Check

One of the strengths of *Relaying the Word* is the accountability factor, which is not as scary as it sounds. It is important to hold each other accountable, because it builds trust and strength.

Before each discussion begins, ask the participants to physically raise their hands if they finished all the reading for that week. Then ask how many were able to finish at least half of it. Be sure to not rush this time and take a moment to allow participants to look around the room and take inventory.

The accountability check is not a time to cast judgment. Life happens, and perhaps someone was not able to finish the reading because he or she had a personal emergency that week. It is the Holy Spirit's job to convict our hearts—not people's.

4. Summary of Reading

There is no doubt that God will speak to everyone during their reading. Some participants will be eager to share, and others will be more private. A good way to open the discussion is to ask the group whether anyone had any *aha!* moments or revelations they would like to report.

Once everyone has an opportunity to share, start going through the prescribed reading a few chapters at a time. Point out any "Jesus references" in the Old Testament as you go along. Also use the guide questions as needed to ignite discussion. Refer to the additional information in the appendix to supplement the discussion.

Each group who goes through this Bible study has a different personality with diverse preferences and beliefs. Find the flow of discussion that best suits your group's needs.

5. Closing Prayer

The closing prayer is equally important as the opening one. Again—find a volunteer in advance. Following are some things to pray for in addition to any specific prayer needs that arise during the discussion.

- Thank God for His Word and revelation.
- Ask the Holy Spirit to seal all the revelations in people's spirits so that the enemy does not come quickly to steal it.

Relaying the Word

- Ask for supernatural time efficiency for the next week's reading.
- Ask for safety in traveling home.

The following sections give a week-by-week breakdown for how to conduct the Bible study.

Relaying the Word

Informational Meeting

Week 1 is the informational meeting and gives a general introduction to the Bible study. Following are the orders of business.

1. Describe the purpose of the Bible study.
The purpose of this Bible study is to learn the Word of God together so that we can run our race to win.

2. Introduce participants.
Go around the room and have everyone introduce themselves and share a few interesting facts about their lives.

3. Describe commitment of the Bible study.
This Bible study is sixteen weeks in length and is composed of one week of introduction, thirteen weeks of reading, and two weeks of catchup.

When doing the study, each participant commits to read approximately twelve pages a day of the Bible, then gather with fellow participants once a week. The weekly meetings provide insight, accountability, fellowship, and encouragement.

4. Describe the general flow of each meeting.
A typical meeting includes fellowship, prayer, and a review/discussion of the week's prescribed reading. The length of each meeting will vary, but commonly will comprise an hour of food and fellowship time followed by an hour of discussion. Following is an example: Each Monday, the group will meet at 6:00 p.m. for an optional carry-in dinner, then will start the Bible study at 7:00 p.m.

5. Finalize the schedule and location.
Set start date, meeting time, and location. The Bible study is scheduled for sixteen weeks; however, each group should take into account holidays, vacations among the participants, and the potential for inclement weather. The sixteen weeks includes two weeks of catchup time. While these are scheduled for Weeks 7 and 13, the group should shift these weeks as needed. If meetings are to be held in different locations each time, also include this information in the schedule. Use the *Schedule of Reading* located in the appendix as a guide.

6. Assign leaders for each meeting.
For best results, identify two leaders per meeting: one to lead the discussion and another to referee (not for any fights or arguments, but mostly to keep all the "chatty" people on task). If different leaders are to be assigned each week, be sure to capture this information in the schedule. The leaders are meant to be instruments for the Bible study, and not teachers.

The leaders must keep the discussion focused on the current reading and not on future readings or doctrinal issues. If the discussion takes on an opinion-fest slant, the leaders need to shift it back to the literal Word and suggest that the participants engage in a private and separate conversation at a later time. For doctrinal disagreements, the leaders should encourage the group to go deeper into the Word on their own time after the Bible study is over and to confer with their pastor for help.

7. Explain directions for each reading.
Choose a Bible version. During this study, you are welcome to read whichever Bible version you prefer. Keep in mind, though, that this Bible study and the prescribed readings are based on a Protestant Bible, not a Catholic one. If you are used to reading only one version, try reading different versions to gain additional insight and open up new perspectives. If you find the King James Version confusing or difficult to read, try a different version. A quick Internet-based review of Bible versions will reveal which versions most Bible scholars agree are acceptable. In the appendix you can find *Information about Bible Versions* to help you decide which version is best for you during this study.

Choose how to "read." While most participants choose to read the text during this Bible study, others choose to listen to an audio version instead. This is a good option for those who struggle to read or who read too slowly to keep up. Also, listening to an audio version is a good option for those who don't have hours to devote to reading. It can be a simple fix to listen to the prescribed reading while driving to work or doing other chores. The key to completing this Bible study is to find what works best for you.

Read with a new mind. To better hear from the Lord, it is strongly suggested that you read with an open mind that is free from doctrinal beliefs and information gleaned from previously heard sermons.

Take notes. As you read or listen to the prescribed reading for the week, make a note of what spoke to you in the reading, every mention or resemblance of Jesus, any *aha!* moments, and what you learned.

Don't go back. Start with the prescribed reading each week and do not go back to grab any unfinished reading from the week before. If you don't finish a reading, save the unread text for the next catchup week.

Use the extra helps in the appendix. Included in the appendix are visual aids and extra helps to make the information easier to digest.

8. Set your expectations.

It is important to set expectations for the Bible study in advance. By doing this, participants get more out of the study and are not caught off guard by the enemy's tactics during it. Based on experience, following are some things to expect before, during, and after the study.

Before:
Do not be surprised to receive opposition from friends and family who may question why you would attempt to read the entire Bible in sixteen weeks. You may have to deal with statements such as: "That's just too much reading"; "There's no way you could get anything out of reading the Bible that fast"; "There's not enough time for reflection on what you read"; "How are you going to fit this in with everything else you do?" etc.

Set it in your mind that you *will* accomplish this Bible study and you *will* comprehend what you read. Do not be intimidated by the speed at which it goes or be afraid of getting left behind. If you fall behind—that's okay and that is what the catchup weeks are for. Don't let the enemy convince you that you cannot do it.

During:
Stay on guard for unexpected emergencies and distractions. The enemy does not want us to read the Word of God and learn how to be victorious over him, and as such, he will do everything possible to keep us from reading. He will come to steal, kill, and destroy our time. The very minute we finally find a moment and a quiet place to read, he uses one of his trickiest tactics—to convince us that we are too tired to read and we need a quick nap instead. If you fall behind or get discouraged, don't let the enemy persuade you to drop out and try again the next time the study is offered. Pray in advance against the enemy's ploys.

Expect that God will speak to you and everyone in the group through His Word. Expect to notice a difference in your life and way of thinking, because the Word renews the mind. Do not be surprised if you or others in the group are healed from old emotional hurts or unforgiveness. Pray for one another, and don't be so rigid that the class cannot stop for a few minutes to pray for someone who was just wiped out with an awesome revelation or who maybe just heard God speak to them for the first time. Also, there may be unbelievers in your group who get saved or backsliders who rededicate their lives to God.

The first few meetings are usually quiet and may resemble pulling teeth to get folks to talk. Usually, by the third meeting, though, everyone is all-in. The more robust the fellowship time is before the meetings, the more relaxed and open the participants will be during the discussions. Don't skimp on the fellowship or cut short its time.

After:
Immediately after finishing the Bible study, you will have a mixture of feelings. On the one hand, you may grieve

because the study is over and you find yourself already missing your new friends, but on the other hand, you may have a sense of accomplishment and a renewed sense of freedom and refreshment, like you might feel on an early spring day. One thing is for sure: You will feel like you have more spare time because you will not have the pressure of reading all the time. On the flip side, you will likely have a new love of the Word and a desire to go deeper in it.

The Word of God says that those to whom much has been given, much will also be demanded, and from the one who has been entrusted with much, more will be asked (see Luke 12:48). Now that you know the Word of God, expect a higher level of accountability in your life.

Genesis through Exodus

Genesis describes Creation and the stories of Noah, Abraham, and Moses.

Exodus describes how the Israelites left Egypt and embarked on their journey to the Promised Land, led by Moses.

Helps Located in the Appendix

- Measurements
- Feasts and Special Holidays
- Layout of the Tabernacle and Israelite Camp

Jesus Finds

- Genesis 1:26: Let "us" make man in our image.
- Genesis 3:15: Jesus defeated Satan.
- Genesis 3:22: The man has become like "one of us" knowing good from evil.
- Genesis 6:16: There was only one door on the ark (that saved earth's inhabitants) like Jesus (who saved mankind) is the only way to heaven.

- Genesis 11:7: Let "us" go down.
- Genesis 14:18: Melchizedek was a type of Jesus.
- Genesis 22:13: Jesus was our ram.
- Genesis 49:10: Until "He" comes to whom it belongs.
- Exodus 12:13: Jesus is the blood that covers us.
- Exodus 12:46: Jesus was our Passover lamb and His bones were not broken.
- Exodus 22:29: Jesus was the First Fruit offering.
- Exodus 30:17–21: We are to be washed in the blood of Christ before we can approach the throne.

Questions to Ignite Discussion

1. What was the first commandment/duty (see Genesis 1:28) and first job assignment (see Genesis 1:19–20) listed in the Bible? What does this say about God's expectations for our lives?

2. Describe the subtle steps that the serpent took in Genesis 3:1–5 to persuade Eve to sin.

3. How did Noah respond to his calling from God (see Genesis 6:22)?

4. What did Noah first do after coming out of the Ark (see Genesis 8:20)? What do his actions say about how we should come out of the storms in our own lives?

5. Genesis 14:20 is the first mention of tithing. Where else in this week's reading is tithing mentioned?

6. How did Abraham respond to his calling from God (see Genesis 12:4)?

7. How did it make you feel to see Abraham trying to bargain with God in Genesis 18:26–33? What does God's response tell you about Him?

Relaying the Word

8. Much lying and deceit was passed down through the generations of Abraham. For example, Abraham lied about his wife to Pharaoh (see Genesis 12:13) and Abimelech (see Genesis 20:2), and Isaac lied about his wife to Abimelech (see Genesis 26:7). What does this say about God's plans and how He uses imperfect people for His perfect plan? Also, what does it say about how unaddressed sin in our lives could affect our children and grandchildren?

9. God spoke to many people through dreams. How were the dreams regarded?

10. Abram, Sarai, and Jacob each got new names. How does this compare with the new identity we get with salvation through Jesus?

11. How is Joseph's life a picture of how God can use the bad things in our lives to make good things (see Genesis 50:20 and Romans 8:28)?

12. What was Moses' response to his calling from God (see Exodus 3)?

13. Sometimes God brings us slowly into a season of our lives instead of doing so instantly. What does Exodus 23:29 say about this approach?

14. Exodus 30:1–11 is an Old Testament mention of the gifts of the Spirit. Why did God fill these certain people with His Spirit, and what did the Spirit allow them to do?

15. Even the greatest of God's leaders are still susceptible to human error and faults. Discuss the incident with Moses described in Exodus 14:13–15, and the incident with Aaron described in Exodus 32:24.

16. The people could tell when Moses had spent time with God (see Exodus 34:29–35). When we spend time with Him, what should we look like?

Leviticus through Deuteronomy 23

Leviticus describes details about the feasts, laws, and ceremonies.

Numbers gives more details about the feasts, laws, and ceremonies, and describes key events during the forty years the Israelites spent in the desert.

Deuteronomy presents several speeches given by Moses to prepare the people to enter the Promised Land. He describes the key events over the forty years they spent in the desert and charges the Israelites to remember what the Lord had done for them, to keep the law, and to teach their children all of these things.

Helps Located in the Appendix

- Measurements
- Feasts and Special Holidays
- Layout of the Tabernacle and Israelite Camp

Jesus Finds

- Leviticus 16:27: Jesus was taken out of the city to Golgotha.
- Leviticus 17:12: Jesus' blood made atonement for us.
- Numbers 9:12: None of Jesus' bones were broken.
- Numbers 21:8: Jesus was the embodiment of sin on the cross, and when we look to it as our salvation, we are saved.
- Numbers 24:17: Jesus was the star that came out of Jacob and the scepter that rose out of Israel.
- Deuteronomy 10:17: Jesus is the Lord of lords.
- Deuteronomy 21:22: Jesus was hung on a wooden cross and was left on it overnight.

Questions to Ignite Discussion

1. List the laws that were surprising to you. Discuss how it is impossible to go even one day without sinning according to the law. What does this say about our need for a Savior?

2. What does Leviticus 6:13 say about our offerings or worship to the Lord? Is there room to be lukewarm?

3. God used the feasts and the theme of redemption to cultivate the Israelite's thinking and prepare them for their coming Messiah. How did these ceremonies and themes point to Jesus?

4. In Leviticus 26:18, 24, and 28, how many times will God punish people for sin? (Keep this in mind for the later discussion about the book of Revelation.)

5. If the layout of the camp as described in Numbers 2 is drawn out on paper, what shape will it be? (Hint: See the *Layout of the Israelite Camp* section in the appendices.)

Relaying the Word

6. What does the constant moving of the camp and tabernacle say about the unity of the Israelites?

7. List all the purposes of the trumpets as described in Numbers 10:1–10. (Keep this in mind for the later discussion about the book of Revelation.)

8. How long was the Lord's arm when He reached down for you (see Numbers 11:23)?

9. Why were the Israelites made to wander in the desert for forty years (see Numbers 14:26–35)? What was their response and then the consequences of it (see Numbers 14:39–45)?

10. What does Numbers 15:30–31 say about the times we knowingly and purposely sin?

11. Numbers 16 tell a story about dissention in leadership. What does God's response to the situation tell you about what He thinks about division in leadership and ministry?

12. Why was Moses not permitted to cross over into the Promised Land (see Numbers 20:12)? What was so wrong about what he did? What was Moses' response to God's punishment (see Deuteronomy 3:23–26)?

13. Balaam was hired by Balak to curse the Israelites; however, God would not permit him to do so, and each time Balaam ended up blessing the people (see Numbers 22–24). How did Balaam and Balak go around God to bring destruction upon the Israelites (see Numbers 31:15–16 and then Numbers 25:1–3)?

14. What does Deuteronomy 6:5–7 say our Christian life should look like behind the closed doors of our homes?

Relaying the Word

Deuteronomy 24 through 1 Samuel

Deuteronomy presents several speeches given by Moses to prepare the people to enter the Promised Land. He describes the key events over their forty years in the desert and charges the Israelites to remember what the Lord has done for them, to keep the law, and to teach their children all of these things.

Joshua tells about the adventures of Israelites as Joshua led them in conquering the Promised Land.

Judges describes several judges who ruled over the Israelites after the death of Joshua and before the kingship of Saul.

Ruth is a story about a kinsman-redeemer who later became the great-grandfather of David.

First Samuel provides the background story of how Saul and David were called and anointed to be king.

Relaying the Word

Helps Located in the Appendix

- Measurements
- Layout of the Tabernacle and Israelite Camp
- Feasts and Special Holidays

Jesus Finds

- Deuteronomy 31:10: On this day, during the drawing of the water ceremony, Jesus told the crowd to let anyone who was thirsty come to Him and drink (see John 7:37).
- Joshua 2:21: The scarlet cord resembles the blood over the door at Passover and the blood of Jesus applied to our lives.
- Ruth 4:14: Jesus is our Kinsman-Redeemer.
- 1 Samuel 2:25: Jesus sits at the right hand of God and intercedes for us.
- David is a type of Jesus.

Questions to Ignite Discussion

1. What were the conditions for receiving the blessings described in Deuteronomy 28:1–14 or the curses described in Deuteronomy 28:15–68?

2. According to Deuteronomy 30:11–19, how important are our words in terms of the kind of lives we will have? If the Lord created the world with His words, and if His Holy Spirit dwells in us, then how powerful are our words in creating life or death for ourselves? What kind of an effect can the careless words we speak over ourselves have (i.e., "I'll never be able to do that"; "It was that way for my parents, so it will be that way for me"; "I'll always be stuck here"; "I'll never succeed"; etc.)?

3. The Israelites often set up stones to be an evidence and a reminder of God's miracles and goodness (see Joshua 4:8–9 as an example). What kind of "stones" should we

Relaying the Word

be leaving for future generations as a legacy and a testimony of God in our lives? Is a tombstone the only "stone" you will leave?

4. The Israelites spent forty years waiting to see the Promised Land; however, when they finally entered in, the manna stopped, they had to eat from the land, and they had to battle for at least five years. How do you think the reality of their situation compared with their expectation of entering a land flowing with milk and honey? How is this conflict of reality versus expectation similar for new Christians who think that once they accept Christ, their lives will be easy and their troubles will disappear?

5. How was Jericho like a firstfruit offering (see Deuteronomy 26:1 and Joshua 6:17)?

6. What was Gideon's response when God called him (see Judges 6:11–15)? How many times did Gideon ask for confirmation from the Lord (see Judges 6:17, 36–40)?

7. How is the story of Ruth and Boaz tied to the lineage of Jesus? How is Jesus our Kinsman-Redeemer?

8. What was Saul's response to his calling (see 1 Samuel 10:21–22)? How do we try to hide behind our own "baggage" when God asks us to do something?

9. According to 1 Samuel 15:22, which is better—obedience or sacrifice? Why?

10. What was David's response to Saul continuously trying to kill him? Why did David not retaliate?

11. When David and his army conquered the Amalekites, he divided the plunder between the men who stayed behind and protected the supplies with the ones who went into battle (see 1 Samuel 30:24). How is this way

of thinking similar to the relationship between intercessory prayer and mission work? If we are not the ones going into the battlefields ourselves, then what should we be doing?

12. In 1 Samuel 13:7–14, we learn how Saul became impatient and took things into his own hands. In 2 Samuel 5:24–25, we see an example of one of the many times that David waited on the Lord before acting. What can we learn from these stories and how can we apply them to our lives?

13. When David was exposed for killing Uriah, what was his response (see 2 Samuel 12:13)? How do we respond when we get caught doing something wrong?

2 Samuel through 2 Kings

Second Samuel tells the stories about the life of David during his kingship.

First Kings describes the transfer of the kingship from David to Solomon and then to later kings after the kingdom became divided into Judah and Israel.

Second Kings presents the evolvement of the kingdoms as the kings interacted with various key prophets (i.e., Elijah and Elisha).

Helps Located in the Appendix

- Measurements
- Layout of the Tabernacle and Israelite Camp
- Feasts and Special Holidays
- Kings and Prophets of Judah and Israel

Jesus Finds

- 2 Samuel 14:14: Jesus is the plan to return mankind to God.
- 2 Kings 4:43: Jesus performed a similar miracle.

Relaying the Word

Questions to Ignite Discussion

1. When the man arrived from Saul's camp and told David about Saul's death, what was David's response (see 2 Samuel 1)? What does this tell us about respecting those whom God has placed in authority over us?

2. Describe the events that took place to bring the Ark of the Covenant back to Jerusalem (see 2 Samuel 6). How did the first attempt differ from the second one?

3. Why was Absalom able to assert himself as king (see 2 Samuel 15)? What was David's response to this? What was the end result?

4. What happened as a result of David's counting of the fighting men (see 2 Samuel 24)? What can we learn from his reply in verse 24?

5. What was Solomon doing when he received the gift of wisdom (see 1 Kings 3:5)? What did he do when he realized that he was dreaming? What does this say about the importance of dreams to God's people?

6. When Solomon dedicated the Temple, what three types of people did he pray for (see 1 Kings 8:30, 8:33, and 8:41)?

7. What was Solomon's downfall (see 1 Kings 11:3–6)? What does this say about the influence that others around us have on us?

8. When Rehoboam was made king, what type of management style did he decide to rule the people with (see 1 Kings 12:13–14)? What resulted from it?

9. What was Jeroboam's first big mistake (see 1 Kings 12:28–30)? Why did he do this?

Relaying the Word

10. Describe the confrontation of Elijah with Jezebel's prophets (see 1 Kings 18). What kind of faith did Elijah demonstrate?

11. God speaks to us in many ways. Describe how He spoke to Elijah in 1 Kings 19:11–12.

12. Describe how Elisha was called (see 1 Kings 19:19–21). What did Elisha's action in verse 21 say about his commitment to serve the Lord?

13. Describe the plans that God gave Elisha to overcome the Moabites (see 2 Kings 3:16–19). Were the plans logical? What was the result? How many times do we disregard the instructions and strategies from God because they don't sound logical? Did Namaan struggle with this same thing (see 2 Kings 5:9–12)?

14. After God told Hezekiah that He would heal him, Hezekiah went ahead with the therapy that Isaiah prepared (see 2 Kings 20:7). What does this say about healing as a miraculous event compared with healing as a process? Does God use both methods? Does it mean that someone is less faithful and doesn't believe their healing is real if they go ahead with a medical treatment?

15. How did Babylon come to know the extent of the Israelite wealth that consequently made them a target for acquisition (see 2 Kings 20:12–15)?

16. What discovery enabled Josiah to lead the people away from other gods and toward their one true God (see 2 Kings 12:8)? Until this rediscovery, the people did not know or hear about the Word of God. What was the people's response when they finally heard the Word of

God for themselves? How is this Bible reading group like a modern-day Josiah generation?

1 Chronicles through Nehemiah

First Chronicles describes the history of the Israelite tribes and David's kingship.

Second Chronicles describes the history of the kings of Judah.

Ezra tells the story of the first Israelites returning from captivity in Babylon and their priest, Ezra, who led the rebuilding and rededication of the Temple.

Nehemiah describes the rebuilding of Jerusalem's wall in fifty-two days.

Helps Located in the Appendix

- Measurements
- Layout of the Tabernacle and Israelite Camp
- Feasts and Special Holidays
- Kings and Prophets of Judah and Israel

Jesus Finds

- 1 Chronicles 11:17: Jesus is the water that eternally satisfies our thirst (see John 4:13).
- 1 Chronicles 17:11-14: Jesus is the Son whose kingdom is forever.

Questions to Ignite Discussion

1. Describe Jabez's prayer in 1 Chronicles 4:9-10. What does this say about the power of simple prayers? What kind of man was Jabez, and do you think his heart had anything to do with God's response?

2. What was David's demeanor when he was bringing the Ark of the Covenant back to Jerusalem (see 1 Chronicles 15:29)? What can we learn about his radical worship? What was Michal's reaction to David's worship and what was her punishment for judging it (see 2 Samuel 6:21-23).

3. First Chronicles 22:14 provides a glimpse of how much David had stockpiled for the building of the Temple. If the gold alone was in the form of today's standard gold bar and was laid end to end, it would be thirty-three miles long and take eleven hours to walk past. How does this affect your thoughts about the dedication and value that David had for the Temple?

4. Because it may be difficult to read through the genealogy and the long lists of names, we may sometimes find ourselves skimming or even skipping these sections of the Word. Second Chronicles 29:12-14 describes the name of the priests who purified the Temple and is a place where deeper revelation can be obtained from the names.

   Mahath means "grasping."

Relaying the Word

Joel means "Jehovah is God."
Kish means "bent."
Azariah means "Jehovah has helped."
Joah means "Jehovah is brother."
Eden means "pleasure."
Shimri means "vigilant."
Jeiel means "God sweeps away."
Zechariah means "Jehovah remembers."
Mattaniah means "gift of Jehovah."
Jehiel means "God lives."
Shemaiah means "heard by Jehovah."
Uzziel means "my strength is God."

If we read the list in order by the meanings of the names, it would sound something like this: *Grasp Jesus as God. He bent down to help you. He is pleased to be your Brother. He will be vigilant to sweep away sin. Remember His free gift. He lives and is great. He hears and is your strength.* What can we learn from this about the layers of revelation that are available in God's Word? How does this demonstrate that every time we read the Bible, we can get a fresh word from the Lord?

5. What tactics did the enemy use as an attempt to stop the rebuilding of the Temple (see Ezra 4:4–6)? How does the enemy use these tactics on us today?

6. How did the Israelites demonstrate unity in Ezra 10:12 and 16–17?

7. What three things did Nehemiah, who was the king's cupbearer, ask of the king in Nehemiah 2:5 and 7–8? How did this show great bravery on Nehemiah's part? What had Nehemiah done prior to the request (see Nehemiah 1:4)?

8. Describe how the men worked amidst great opposition from the surrounding villages (see Nehemiah 4:16–18).

Relaying the Word

How can we apply this approach to our own lives when trouble comes against us?

9. How many days did it take to complete the wall (see Nehemiah 6:15–16)? What effect did this have on the surrounding enemies? How can the testimony of God working in our lives do the same?

Catchup Week

NO MEETING!!

Esther through Psalm 89

The book of Esther describes how a young Jewish girl became a queen in Persia and how she used her new position to save the Jewish people from slaughter.

The book of Job describes how a faithful man who suffered great personal loss at the hands of the enemy came to know God in a new way.

Psalms is a collection of prayers, hymns, and worship that covers nearly every emotional situation known to man.

Helps Located in the Appendix

- Feasts and Special Holidays

Jesus Finds

- Job 9:33–34: Jesus is our arbitrator in heaven and His death removed the punishment from us.
- Job 16:19: Jesus is our witness and intercessor in heaven.
- Job 19:25: Jesus is our Redeemer and He lives.

- Job 33:24, 28: Jesus ransomed us and spared us from going down into the pit of hell.

The book of Psalms has too many to list, so only the really obvious ones are included here.

- Psalm 2:2: Jesus is the Anointed One.
- Psalm 14:7: Jesus is our salvation that came out of Zion.
- Psalm 16:10: Jesus lives and never saw decay.
- Psalm 19:6: Jesus sits at the right hand of God and is His saving power.
- Psalm 22:1: These were part of Jesus' last words on the cross (see Matthew 27:46 and Mark 15:34).
- Psalm 22:12–18: This describes the crucifixion of Jesus.
- Psalm 31:5: These were Jesus' last words on the cross (see Luke 23:46).
- Psalm 34:20: None of Jesus' bones were broken.
- Psalm 45: Jesus is our Bridegroom.
- Psalm 49:7–9: Only Jesus, the Son of God, can do this.
- Psalm 69:8–9: These are the costs that Jesus described in Luke 14:26 and Mark 10:28–30.
- Psalm 69:21: Jesus was given a sponge filled with vinegar while He was on the cross (see Matthew 27:48, Mark 15:36, Luke 23:36, and John 19:29).
- Psalm 72:1–2: Jesus is the Son of God who will judge us.
- Psalm 78:1–2: Jesus spoke in parables.
- Psalm 88: This describes what Jesus may have felt when He was in the pit awaiting crucifixion.
- Psalm 89:27–29: Jesus is the firstborn whose line will be established forever.

Relaying the Word

Questions to Ignite Discussion

1. What does the story of Esther tell us about how God can place His people in seemingly unattainable positions to accomplish His will?

2. Haman was an Agagite (descendant of Agag, the king of the Amalekites, whom God ordered the Israelites to annihilate; see 1 Samuel 15). What does this teach us about not following through with instructions from God and the potential consequences that may later arise?

3. Through obedience and patience, Esther allowed herself to be placed in the correct position and time for God to use her "for such a time as this" (Esther 4:14). How can we apply this story to our own lives?

4. What was Job's regular custom (see Job 1:4–5)? Do you think it could have become a routine?

5. Who was afflicting Job? Whom did Job say was afflicting him (see Job 6:4, 8; 13:15; 16:9; 19:6, 8–13)? What does Job accuse God of doing in 19:9? In 13:15 and 30:21–23? In 10:8?

6. Job accuses God of being unjust. What was Job's opinion of himself (see 27:6; 32:1; 33:9; 34:5)? In Job 31, he justifies himself and his actions, but what was God's opinion about it all (see Job 40:8)? When God set Job straight, what was Job's response (see 42:3)?

7. Who was Elihu, and how did he differ from Job's other three friends?

8. What did Elihu say about Job in 34:35? How does this compare with the words God spoke when He came on the scene (see 38:2)? Did Job really know God? Before his trial, did Job have religion or a relationship? What about afterward (see 42:5)?

9. Compare and contrast how Job and David knew God and the relationship each one had with Him. How did each describe God's justice?

10. Did David have religion or a relationship with God? How do we know?

11. How are sin and sickness related, as described in Psalm 38?

12. David knew from a young age that he was anointed to be king, yet he had to wait patiently for his time. Even he had to come to a point of surrendering to the Lord's will before he could step into his calling. What does Psalm 40:7–8 reveal about this moment?

Psalm 90 through Isaiah 13

Psalms is a collection of prayers, hymns, and worship that covers nearly every emotional situation known to man.

Proverbs offers advice about various aspects of life and provides wisdom.

Ecclesiastes evaluates the meaning of life without God.

Song of Songs is a book of romance and reminds us of how much God loves us.

Isaiah was written by the prophet Isaiah who saw the many troubles in the surrounding nations and pointed to a coming Messiah.

Helps Located in the Appendix

- Kings and Prophets of Judah and Israel

Jesus Finds

The book of Psalms has too many to list, so only the really obvious ones are included here.

- Psalm 106:23: Moses was a type of Jesus, who stood in our gap.
- Psalm 107:20: Jesus is the Word who was sent to heal and rescue us.
- Psalm 107:28–29: Jesus calmed the seas (see Matthew 8:23–27, Mark 4:35–41, and Luke 8:22–25).
- Psalms 109:31 and 110:1: Jesus sits at the right hand of God.
- Psalm 110:4: Jesus is our forever priest in the order of Melchizedek (see Hebrews 5:10, and several other places in Hebrews 6 and 7).
- Psalm 111:9: Jesus is the means for our redemption.
- Psalm 118:22: Jesus is the stone the builders rejected (see Matthew 21:42, Mark 12:10, and Luke 20:17).
- Proverbs 8:22–36: This describes Jesus.
- Proverbs 18:24: Jesus is our friend who sticks closer than a brother.
- Proverbs 27:6: Jesus was betrayed by Judas's kiss (see Luke 22:48).
- Proverbs 30:4: Jesus is His name.
- Song of Songs: In general, the Church is the beloved and Jesus is the Lover.
- Song of Songs 3:6: Jesus could be smelled as He came into town (see John 12:3, 12).
- Isaiah 9:1: This is a prophecy that Jesus fulfilled describing where the Messiah would come from.
- Isaiah 9:2: This could reference the Star of Bethlehem.
- Isaiah 9:6–7: This describes Jesus.
- Isaiah 11:1–5: This describes Jesus, who came from the lineage of Jesse.

Relaying the Word

Questions to Ignite Discussion

1. What does Psalm 139:13–16 tell us about how well God knows us?

2. What will wisdom do for our path in life (see Proverbs 4:11–12)? How is this Bible study helping with this?

3. What are the seven things that are detestable to God (see Proverbs 6:16–19)?

4. What does Proverbs 13:22 say about the legacy we should leave? Do you think this is referring to wealth only?

5. How does Haman's plight in the book of Esther illustrate Proverbs 26:27?

6. According to Proverbs 31:10–31, what does a wife with noble character look like?

7. How can we apply Ecclesiastes 3:1–8 to the seasons of our lives?

8. If Song of Songs is an illustration of the intimate relationship we should have with God, what does this relationship look like?

9. What does Isaiah 1:18 tell us about how God wants to communicate with us? Does He want us to talk *at* each other or *with* each other?

10. What was Isaiah's response when he encountered the living God in Isaiah 6:5? What was his response when he was called (Isaiah 6:8)?

Relaying the Word

Isaiah 14 through Jeremiah 33

Isaiah was written by the prophet Isaiah, who saw the many troubles in the surrounding nations and pointed to a coming Messiah.

Jeremiah was written by the prophet Jeremiah, who spoke predominantly to Judah in the last decades before the Babylonian invasion of the nation. He continually warned the people to turn back to God.

Helps Located in the Appendix

- Feasts and Special Holidays
- Kings and Prophets of Judah and Israel

Jesus Finds

- Isaiah 16:5: Jesus is the one sitting on this throne.
- Isaiah 28:16: Jesus is the cornerstone.
- Isaiah 40:10–11: Jesus is the Shepherd and brings recompense.
- Isaiah 42:1–4: Jesus endured to bring us justice.
- Isaiah 43:10–13: Jesus is God in the flesh.

Relaying the Word

- Isaiah 50:6: Jesus endured this abuse before the crucifixion.
- Isaiah 52:13–15: A picture of Jesus on the cross.
- Isaiah 53: This chapter is all about Jesus.
- Isaiah 59:16: Jesus is God working out our salvation by His own hands.
- Isaiah 59:20: Jesus is the Redeemer.
- Isaiah 61:1: Jesus came to set us free.
- Jeremiah 7:10: Jesus said this in Matthew 21:13, Mark 11:17, and Luke 19:46.
- Jeremiah 23:5: Jesus is the righteous branch from the lineage of David.
- Jeremiah 31:31: Jesus is the new covenant.
- Jeremiah 33:15–16: Jesus is the righteous branch from the lineage of David.

Questions to Ignite Discussion

1. If Isaiah 14:12–15 describes Lucifer, what is his backstory?

2. What place is Isaiah 24:21–22 describing?

3. What does Isaiah 54:17 say about attacks against us?

4. What does Isaiah 55:11 say about words spoken by God? If we are filled with the Holy Spirit, what does this mean for our words?

5. What does Jeremiah 17:10 teach us about the judgment of our intentions versus our actions?

6. Jeremiah 29:11 describes the plans that God has for our lives. What are they?

Jeremiah 34 through Daniel

Jeremiah was written by the prophet Jeremiah, who spoke predominantly to Judah in the last decades before the Babylonian invasion of the nation. He continually warned the people to turn back to God.

Lamentations describes the sorrow resulting from the Babylonian invasion and how Jeremiah's warnings came to pass.

Ezekiel was written by the prophet Ezekiel, who spoke to the captives in Babylon with words and prophetic deeds.

Daniel tells how he, a captive in Babylon, became the prime minister in the government. This book also expresses the importance of dreams and how God speaks through them.

Helps Located in the Appendix

- Feasts and Special Holidays
- Kings and Prophets of Judah and Israel

Jesus Finds

- Lamentations 3:28–29: Our sin was laid upon Jesus.

Relaying the Word

- Ezekiel 34:22–24: Jesus is our Shephard.
- Daniel 3:25: Jesus is the fourth Person in the fire and goes through trials with us.
- Daniel 7:13–14: This describes a vision of Jesus.

Questions to Ignite Discussion

1. What point is God trying to make in Jeremiah 35:13–14?

2. Lamentations is a very sorrowful book that describes the state of things after the Babylonian invasion; however, it balances the sorrow with bits of hope about the faithfulness of God despite the circumstances. List some instances of hope and peace that are sprinkled throughout the book.

3. If our brothers or sisters backslide and we fail to warn them before they die in their sin, who is accountable (see Ezekiel 3:20–21)?

4. What does Ezekiel 37:1–10 say about our ability to speak to and bring life to dead situations?

5. What does the book of Daniel say about God speaking through dreams?

6. Why was Daniel thrown into the lions' den? What happened while he was in there? What were the end results of Daniel's obedience (see Daniel 6:26–28)?

7. According to Daniel 9:23, how long after we pray is an answer *given*? Do we always *receive* the answer in the same amount of time (see Daniel 10:12–14)? Are we always permitted to fully understand the answer (see Daniel 12:8–9)?

Hosea through Matthew

Hosea describes how God called a prophet to marry an unfaithful wife to illustrate how Israel had been spiritually unfaithful to Him.

Joel foretells God's judgment of Judah.

Amos warns about helping the poor, particularly during a time of prosperity.

Obadiah is a collection of warnings for Edom.

Jonah tells of a prophet who, after facing discipline for his reluctance, warned Nineveh about pending judgment, which caused them to repent and turn back to God.

Micah describes the rampant corruption among the people, but offers promises for forgiveness and restoration if they return to God.

Nahum tells how the prophet preached to Nineveh long after Jonah and foretells of the city's impending destruction for their backsliding.

Relaying the Word

Habakkuk is a conversation between the prophet and God about his frustrations concerning justice.

Zephaniah is about the coming "day of the Lord" and the end-time prophecies against the nations.

Haggai tells how a handful of Jews returned to Jerusalem from the Babylonian captivity to rebuild the Temple.

Zechariah is a continuation of encouragement for the Jews to continue their work on rebuilding the Temple and describes how the Temple will point toward the coming Messiah.

Malachi describes how the nation had once again grown indifferent and warns them to repent and turn back to God.

Matthew was written for the Jews and explains how Jesus is the Messiah promised in the Old Testament.

Helps Located in the Appendix

- Kings and Prophets of Judah and Israel

Jesus Finds

- Hosea 6:2: Jesus was resurrected in three days.
- Jonah 1:17: Jonah was in the belly of the fish as Jesus was in the heart of the earth (the sign Jesus referred to in Matthew 12:39–40).
- Micah 2:13: Jesus is the One who made a way for us.
- Micah 4:2: The Gospel of Jesus went out from Jerusalem.
- Micah 5:2: Jesus came from Bethlehem.
- Micah 5:4: Jesus is our Shepherd and He brings us peace.
- Habakkuk 3:4: This contains a picture of the power of Jesus coming from the nail holes in His hands.
- Zephaniah 1:7: Jesus is our sacrifice.

Relaying the Word

- Zechariah 3:1: Jesus is our High Priest.
- Zechariah 3:8–9: Jesus is the Branch and will remove the sin of the land in one day.
- Zechariah 9:9: Jesus came riding on a donkey.
- Zechariah 11:13: Judas sold out Jesus for thirty pieces of silver (see Matthew 26:15; 27:3–10).
- Zechariah 12:10–14: There is intense mourning for the one they pierced (Jesus).

Questions to Ignite Discussion

1. What were God's instructions to Hosea concerning his unfaithful wife (see Hosea 3:1)? What point was the Lord trying to make?

2. The Lord is the God of restoration. What does Joel 2:25 say about what the enemy has stolen from us?

3. Who was Amos (see Amos 7:14–16)? What does this say about how God uses people in different ways for different seasons of their lives?

4. What does Obadiah 1:15 say about the way we treat others?

5. What was Jonah's response when the Lord instructed him to warn the people of Nineveh? When Nineveh repented, what was Jonah's response?

6. What effect can our disobedience have on those around us (see Jonah 1:12)?

7 What does the Lord require of us (see Micah 7:8)?

8. What will happen to people who use the prophetic gift for their own purposes (see Micah 3:5–7)?

Relaying the Word

9. According to the book of Nahum, what happened to Nineveh years after Jonah's ministry and Nineveh's resulting repentance?

10. What was Habakkuk's first complaint and God's response? His second complaint and the response? What did Habakkuk resolve to do (see Habakkuk 3:16–18)?

11. Zephaniah 3:12–13 describes a remnant of God's people in the last days. What are they like?

12. What does Haggai say about putting the House of God before our own house?

13. According to Zechariah 3:1, who stands before the throne of God to accuse us?

14. In Zechariah 7:4–6, God questions the people about their motives when they fasted and celebrated the holy days. How would we answer that question for ourselves?

15. In Malachi 3:7–8, God says that we rob Him. How so? What is the promise attached to proper tithing and giving (see Malachi 3:10–12)?

16. When Jesus was in the wilderness, what did Satan try to tempt Him with (see Matthew 4:1–11)? What was Jesus' response?

17. According to Matthew 7:21, who will enter the kingdom of heaven?

18. What promise does Jesus make to those who are weary or burdened (see Matthew 11:28–30)?

19. What are our words a reflection of (see Matthew 12:33–37)?

Catchup Week

NO MEETING!!

Relaying the Word

Mark through Acts 6

Mark was likely written for the Romans (Gentiles) and details the events in Jesus' ministry on earth.

Luke describes the events of Jesus' ministry with a joyful and human-interest tone.

John also describes the events of Jesus' ministry, but he does so with more explanation of who Jesus is and why He came.

Acts tells of the events following the resurrection of Jesus and how the Gospel spread.

Questions to Ignite Discussion

1. According to Mark 12:29–31, what is the greatest commandment?

2. Is it enough to have faith and believe when we pray, or is there something else we need to do (see Mark 11:23)?

3. What was Mary's response when she heard the shepherds declaring who Jesus was (see Luke 2:19)? What did she not do?

Relaying the Word

4. What does Luke 12:48 tell us about accountability?

5. In John 8:32–31, Jesus said, "If you hold to my teaching, you are really my disciples." What is the result of doing this?

6. What does the enemy come to do, as described in John 10:10?

7. Why was Caiaphas (the high priest) vying for the death of Jesus (see John 11:49–53)?

8. What happened at Pentecost, as described in the book of Acts?

Acts 7 through 2 Thessalonians

Acts tells of the events following the resurrection of Jesus and how the gospel spread.

Romans is a letter written by Paul to explain theology and how it works in Christian living.

First Corinthians is a letter written by Paul to provide practical insight of how to live a Christian life despite problems.

Second Corinthians is a letter written by Paul to defend himself against accusations.

Galatians is a letter written by Paul to address legalism.

Ephesians is a letter written by Paul to encourage believers and tell of the advantages of living a Christian life.

Philippians is a letter written by Paul to encourage and thank believers for their faithfulness.

Colossians is a letter written by Paul to encourage believers to stick to the teachings of the Gospel and not be swayed by false religions.

Relaying the Word

First Thessalonians is a letter written by Paul to encourage believers to keep the faith and live for God.

Second Thessalonians covers much the same topics as 1 Thessalonians, and warns against lawlessness and idleness.

Questions to Ignite Discussion

1. According to Acts 4:12, how are we saved?

2. Who was Saul, and what was his relationship with the early Christians? What changed him?

3. What happened to the unbelievers who tried to act with the authority of the name of Jesus (see Acts 19:13–16)?

4. We read in Jeremiah that God knew us before He created us and that we were created for a purpose. What does Acts 17:26 say about when and where He decided to place us?

5. What does Acts 20:24 encourage us to do?

6. What can we gain from our sufferings, according to Romans 5:3–5?

7. How does the Holy Spirit help us pray (see Romans 8:26–27)?

8. What must we do to be saved (see Romans 10:9)? Is it enough to just say we are Christians? If we truly believe, then what should our lives and actions look like?

9. If someone is not a Christian and does not have the Holy Spirit, should we expect them to understand why or how we believe (see 1 Corinthians 2:14)?

10. According to 1 Corinthians 10:13, will Christians have to deal with temptations?

Relaying the Word

11. Discuss some of the spiritual gifts and roles in the kingdom, as described in 1 Corinthians 12.

12. Should we be the same creature after we are saved (see 2 Corinthians 5:17)?

13. How do Christians wage war (see 2 Corinthians 10:12–15)?

14. The Bible says that we are to bear fruit in our life (see John 15:8). What are the fruits of the Spirit (see Galatians 5:22)?

15. Describe the armor of God listed in Ephesians 6.

16. The Bible tells us to take captive every thought (2 Corinthians 10:5) and to renew our minds (Romans 12:2). According to Philippians 4:8, what kind of thoughts should we concentrate on?

17. Should we work to please man or God in all we do (see Colossians 3:24)? Whom are we really working for?

18. Paul kept telling others that he would be persecuted, and he certainly was (see 1 Thessalonians 3:4). What can we learn about the words we speak over our own lives?

19. What does Paul say about idleness in 2 Thessalonians 3? What are the two types of groups that people fall into (see 2 Thessalonians 3:11)?

Relaying the Word

1 Timothy through Revelation

First Timothy is a letter written by Paul to serve as a manual for young ministers.

Second Timothy is a letter written by Paul to give his final words before death.

Titus is a letter written by Paul to teach how to disciple believers and young churches.

Philemon is a letter written by Paul to ask Philemon to forgive his slave. It is a picture of Jesus requesting our freedom.

Hebrews warns against slipping back into Judaism and explains how many events and prophecies in the Old Testament pointed toward Jesus.

James spells out the specifics of how to be a real Christian in actions and not just in words.

First Peter encourages Christians who are being persecuted for their faith.

Relaying the Word

Second Peter deals with problems in the Church and warns against false teachers.

First John gives the basic truths of Christian life.

Second John warns against false teachers and tells how to deal with them.

Third John is a complement to 2 John and teaches us to be hospitable to true teachers.

Jude tells how to deal with godless people.

Revelation is a prophetic book written by John that describes end-time events and the final battle between good and evil.

Helps Located in the Appendix

- Revelation Helps

Questions to Ignite Discussion

1. According to 1 Timothy 2:1–3, what should we be doing for our leaders?

2. What did the Lord give us, according to 2 Timothy 1:17?

3. Titus 2 teaches that we all have something we need to learn. What does this tell us about discipleship?

4. How is Paul's plea for Philemon's freedom similar to Jesus' plea for our freedom?

5. What is faith, according to Hebrews 11:1?

6. Is it enough to just read the Word of God (see James 1:22–25)?

7. Why do we not always get what we want (see James 4:2–3)?

8. What does 1 Peter say about submission to leaders? To our spouses?

9. Why is the Lord patient with people (see 2 Peter 3:9)?

10. What does 1 John 2:3–6 say about people who talk the talk, but do not walk the walk?

11. How can we be an overcomer (see 1 John 4:4)?

12. What does 2 John say about walking in obedience to the Lord's commands?

13. What does 3 John say about being hospitable to God's faithful people?

14. Describe Jude's call for us to persevere.

15. Today's society resembles the church of Laodicea described in Revelation 3:14–22. How does God feel about lukewarm people?

16. What is promised to those who overcome (see Revelation 2:7; 2:11; 2:17; 2:26–28; 3:5; 3:12; and 3:21)?

17. Describe the seven seals, trumpets, and bowls. (See the timeline and summary in the Revelation Helps section of the appendix.)

18. What is the sealed remnant doing during the end times (see Revelation 7:1–4 and 14:1–5)?

19. What were Jesus' final words to us in Revelation (see 22:7; 22:12–16; and 22:20)?

Relaying the Word

Relaying the Word is a lifetime race.

When we die, only "our" part of the race of life is over; the race itself goes on with the runners who come after us. The same concept is true with this Bible study. Although we may be finished with the study, our assignment is not complete until we pass along and share what we have gained with others. The Great Commission tells us to go and make disciples. After this Bible study, it will be our turn to pass the baton to those coming behind us—and it's a task that will take the remainder of our lifetime and require us to take on many roles.

Sometimes we will continue running as a team player. We can do this by participating in subsequent *Relaying the Word* study groups and helping others to get their groups up and running. We can share our testimonies and draft others to the team. Sometimes our initial sprint through the Bible can turn into a marathon.

Sometimes we will assume the role of team captain and serve as leaders for subsequent *Relaying the Word* study groups. This participation guide can serve as your game plan and help you get off to a great start.

Sometimes we may switch from being a team member or a captain to a coach. The Word of God says that from those who have been given much, much will be demanded; and from the one who has been entrusted with much, more will be asked (Luke 12:48). There comes a time in our lives when we need to take all the knowledge that has been imparted to us and begin to pour it out for others. What starts as a simple Bible study can eventually develop into a ministry of discipleship.

Regardless of whether you are running as an individual or as a team, whether you are a team member, a captain, or a coach, we all must run the race of life together and relay the Word of God.

Appendix: Extra Material to Help with the Readings

Relaying the Word

1. Schedule of Reading

Week	Reading	Discussion Date
1	Introduction to Study	
2	Genesis thru Exodus	
3	Leviticus thru Deuteronomy 23	
4	Deuteronomy 24 thru 1 Samuel	
5	2 Samuel thru 2 Kings	
6	1 Chronicles thru Nehemiah	
7	Catchup	
8	Esther thru Psalm 89	
9	Psalm 90 thru Isaiah 13	
10	Isaiah 14 thru Jeremiah 33	
11	Jeremiah 34 thru Daniel 12	
12	Hosea thru Matthew	
13	Catchup	
14	Mark thru Acts 6	
15	Acts 7 thru 2 Thessalonians	
16	1 Timothy thru Revelation	

2. Additional Online Resources

Bible Gateway (www.biblegateway.com) provides online scripture in a wide variety of Bible versions.

The Blue Letter Bible (www.blueletterbible.org) is an online interactive reference library. One of its key offerings is the Hebrew-Greek lexicon, which gives users immediate access to the original Hebrew and Greek words of each passage, as well as cross-referencing of the original language to other passages throughout the entire Old and New Testament.

The Streaming Bible (http://thestreamingbible.com/) is an online site where you can listen to the Bible for free.

3. Information about Bible Versions

During this study, you are welcome to read whichever Bible version you prefer. Here is some basic information about the most commonly used versions.

King James Version (KJV)

*A word-for-word translation.

*Translation authorized by King James I of England in 1604.

*Preceded by the Geneva Bible.

*All KJV Bibles published before 1666 included the Apocrypha.

*This Bible version is the most widely accepted across all denominations.

*Can be difficult to read and understand.

New King James Version (NKJV)

*A word-for-word translation.

*A revision of the KJV by 130 Bible scholars, Church leaders, and lay Christians.

*Uses modern words but still retains the stylistic beauty of the original KJV.

New International Version (NIV)

*A combination of a word-for-word and thought-for-thought translation.

*An original translation of the Bible developed by more than 100 scholars working from the best available Hebrew, Aramaic, and Greek texts.

New English Translation (NET)

*A combination of word-for-word and thought-for-thought translation.

*An original translation of the Bible, completed by more than twenty-five experts in the original biblical languages who worked directly from the best currently available Hebrew, Aramaic, and Greek texts.

New American Standard Bible (NASB)

*A word-for-word translation.

*The version goal was to render grammar and terminology in contemporary English.

The Message (MSG)

*A thought-for-thought and paraphrase translation.

*The version goal was to recapture scripture in the words we use today.

*Contains no verse numbers.

*Is like reading a story instead of scripture.

*Not well-suited for Bible study, but good to get the gist of what is going on.

Amplified Bible (AMP)

*A combination of word-for-word and thought-for-thought translation.

*Provides multiple English word equivalents to each key Hebrew and Greek words to clarify and "amplify" meanings that may otherwise have been concealed by the traditional translation method.

*Provides alternate meanings of words or phrases in brackets.

*The information in brackets can disrupt flow of reading.

4. Sample Salvation Prayer

Dear heavenly Father,

I accept Jesus Christ as my Savior and my Redeemer. I believe He died for my sins. I ask that my sins be forgiven and that I be washed clean in His blood. I confess that He is Lord and I will live my life serving Him. Amen.

5. Measurements

The following conversions are approximate.

Length

Cubit
18 inches
0.5 meters
52 centimeters

Reed
6 cubits
8.75–10 feet
2.7–3.1 meters

Fathom
4 cubits
6 feet
1.8 meters

Span
3 handbreadths
1.2 cubits
9 inches
23 centimeters

Finger
0.25 handbreadths
0.73 inches
1.85 centimeters

Sabbath Day's Journey
0.6 mile
1 kilometer

Furlong
1/8 mile
660 feet
201.2 meters

Day's Journey
20 miles
32 kilometers

Handbreadth
4 fingers
3 inches
8 centimeters

Long Cubit
7 handbreadths
20 inches

Weight

Bekah
10 gerahs
0.2 ounces
5.5 grams

Gerah
0.02 ounces
0.6 grams

Mina
50 shekels
1.25 pounds
0.6 kilograms

Pim
1.3 bekas
0.66 shekel
0.33 ounces
7.6 grams

Shekel
2 bekas
20 gerahs
0.4 ounces
11.5 grams

Talent
60 minas
3,000 shekels
75 pounds
34 kilograms

Liquid and Dry Measures

Bath
6 hins
1 ephah
6 gallons
22 liters

Ephah
10 omers
0.6 bushels
22 liters

Hin
12 logs
0.17 bath
4 quarts
4 liters

Homer
10 baths
58 gallons
220 liters

Homer (also called Cor)
10 ephaths
6 bushels
220 liters

Cab
4 logs
0.05 ephah
1 quart
1 liter

Lethech
5 ephahs
3 bushels
110 liters

Log
0.3 quart
0.3 liter

Metretes
10–30 gallons
38–115 liters

Omer (also called issaron)
0.1 ephah
2 quarts
2 liters

Seah
2 hins
0.33 ephah
7 quarts
7.3 liters

Money

Didrachma
2 drachma
~0.07 ounce silver
~2 grams silver

Drachma
~0.035 ounce silver
~1 gram silver

Talent, Gold
~120 pounds
~ 54.4 kilograms

Talent, Gold (Alternate)
~60 pounds
~27.2 kilograms

Talent, Silver
~100 pounds
~45.4 kilograms

Talent, Silver (Alternate)
~50 pounds
~22.7 kilograms

Time

Sunrise = 6 a.m.

First hour = 7 a.m.

Second hour = 8 a.m.

Third hour = 9 a.m.

Fourth hour = 10 a.m.

Fifth hour = 11 a.m.

Sixth hour = Noon

Seventh hour = 1 p.m.

Eighth hour = 2 p.m.

Ninth hour = 3 p.m.

Tenth hour = 4 p.m.

Eleventh hour = 5 p.m.

Sunset = 6 p.m.

First watch of night = 6 p.m. to 9 p.m.

Second watch = 9 p.m. to midnight

Third watch = Midnight to 3 a.m.

Fourth watch = 3 a.m. to 6 a.m.

6. Layout of the Tabernacle and Israelite Camp

Layout of the Tabernacle

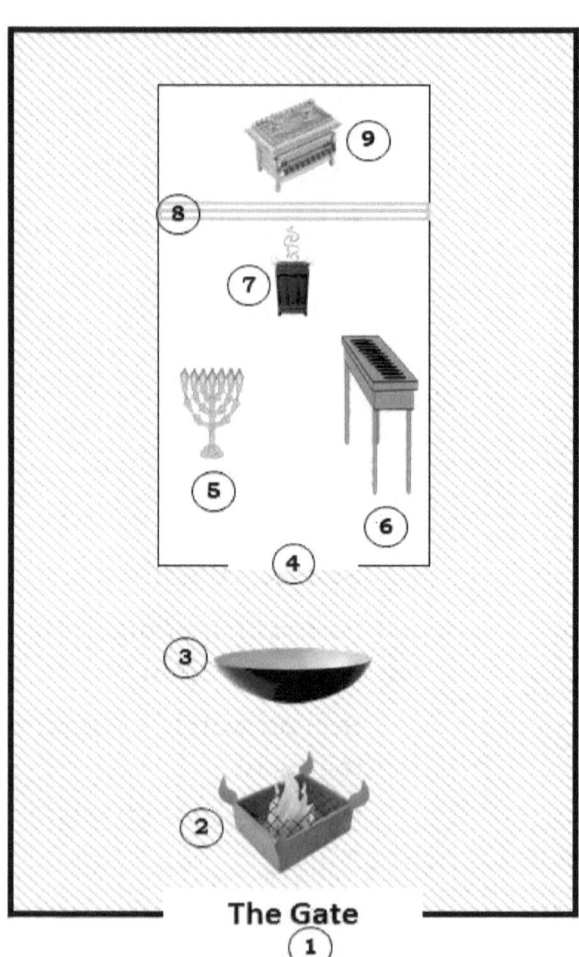

1. The Gate
2. The Brazen Altar
3. The Laver
4. The Entrance to the Holy Place
5. The Lampstand
6. The Table of Shewbread
7. The Altar of Incense
8. The Veil
9. The Ark of the Covenant in the Holy of Holies

Relaying the Word

Layout of the Israelite Camp

```
                        Naphtali

                         Asher

                          Dan

                       ┌─────────┐
                       │ Levites │
Benjamin   Manasseh  Ephraim │   &     │  Judah   Issachar   Zebulun
                       │Tabernacle│
                       └─────────┘

                         Reuben

                         Simeon

                          Gad
```

7. Feasts and Special Holidays

When you plan the timing of the series and the food themes, add a bit of the holidays into your weekly meetings.

This section contains basic information on some Jewish feasts and holidays. Search online for additional information about traditions.

Feasts

Following is a list of the seven feasts instituted by God. Not only were the feasts prophetic rehearsals for the coming of the Messiah, but they were also a foreshadowing of the end-time events.

- *Passover
- *Feast of Unleavened Bread
- *First Fruits
- *Feast of Weeks (Pentecost, the Feast of Harvest, or Shavuot)
- *Feast of Trumpets (Rosh Hashanah)
- *Day of Atonement (Yom Kippur)
- *Feast of Tabernacles (Feast of the Ingathering)

Passover and the Feast of Unleavened Bread

Passover is commemoration of God's deliverance of the Israelites out of Egypt. The Passover was a blood covenant in which blood from a sinless lamb would be payment for death. The Passover lamb was to be killed between the evenings (translated as about 3:00 pm, or the ninth hour).

Passover is the first day of the Feast of Unleavened Bread. For seven days the Israelites were to eat bread made without yeast. Leaven represents sin in one's heart and life, and thus this feast was a reminder to live one's life without sin.

These feasts are celebrated on the 14th to 15th (Passover) and 15th to 22nd (Feast of Unleavened Bread) days of Nisan (usually in March or April).

Prophecy: Passover and Feast of Unleavened Bread was prophecy of the sinless offering of Christ. Jesus was the ultimate Passover lamb. He died when the Passover lamb of the feast was sacrificed (the ninth hour), but unlike the festival lamb, the blood of Jesus is an eternal covering of all who come under it.

End-times: Passover and Feast of Unleavened Bread celebrate death passing over the sealed first born and the coming out of Egypt. Passover draws similarity to the sealing of the 144,000 Jewish people. Whereas, the Feast of Unleavened Bread is a celebration of the rapture of those who are sinless (washed clean in the Blood and thus without leaven).

Feast of First Fruits

The Feast of First Fruits is the only Levitical feast no longer observed in modern Judaism. It was originally a commemoration of God's provision for His people. The Israelites were to celebrate with the first fruits of the crops sown in the field. Today, the Feast of First Fruits is celebrated by Christians and is otherwise known as Easter. This feast was celebrated on the 16th to 17th days of Nisan (usually in March or April).

Prophecy: The Feast of First Fruits was a prophecy of the resurrection of Christ. Christ has indeed been raised from the dead and is the first fruit.

End-times: First Fruits and the Feast of Weeks are similar to the events during the opening of the seven seals. Jesus is first fruit of resurrection. During the period between the first fruits and the Feast of Weeks, the fields are worked and the crops are tended. The cultivation of souls in the end-time events begins with the opening of the seven seals.

Feast of Weeks
Fifty days after Passover begins is the Feast of Weeks, also known as Pentecost, the Feast of Harvest, or Shavuot. According to Rabbinic tradition, the Ten Commandments were given on this day. This feast was a commemoration of God's provision of the Law. As part of the sacrifice, a wave offering of two loaves of bread made with leaven (representing sin) was to be done. This is the only offering in which leaven was allowed. All other offerings were to be sinless. This feast is celebrated on the 6th to 7th days of Sivan (usually in May or June).

Prophecy: The Feast of Weeks (Pentecost) was a prophecy of the coming of the Holy Spirit. The two loaves of bread to be presented as a wave offering were to be made with leaven (representative of sin). The loaves could represent Jews and Gentiles brought together as one in Jesus Christ.

End-times: First Fruits and the Feast of Weeks are similar to the events during the opening of the seven seals. Jesus is first fruit of resurrection. During the period between the first fruits and the Feast of Weeks, the fields are worked and the crops are tended. The cultivation of souls in the end-time events begins with the opening of the seven seals.

Feast of Trumpets
The Feast of Trumpets (Rosh Hashanah) is the commemoration of the New Year. It is announced by the

blowing of trumpets, which is also a call to the Israelite community for assembly. At Rosh Hashanah, the shofar sounds in Synagogues all over the world. The sound of the trumpet is a reminder of the grace God granted Abraham when He supplied him with a sacrificial ram to replace his son Isaac. This feast is celebrated on the 1st day of Tishri (usually in September or October).

Prophecy: The Feast of Trumpets is a prophecy of the second coming of Christ. The trumpets will announce the second coming of Jesus, who will descend from Heaven with a loud command, with the voice of the archangel, and with the trumpet call of God.

End-times: Feast of Trumpets is a proclamation of the Savior. The initial trumpet blast on Rosh Hashanah bears to mind the grace of God and calls people to repentance. In the end times, it announces the second coming of Jesus and also presents a call to repentance. For ten days after Rosh Hashanah (known as the Ten Days of Awe) the people repent. These ten days are like the next six trumpets blowing.

Day of Atonement

The Day of Atonement (Yom Kippur) is a commemoration of the need for atonement. It is preceded by the Ten Days of Awe and is a period of repentance initiated by the sounding of the trumpet on Rosh Hashanah. During the Ten Days of Awe, the Israelites are to consider their ways and turn their hearts toward God. A change of heart must first take place before the redeeming sacrifices of Yom Kippur can be accepted.

According to tradition, Yom Kippur is considered the date on which Moses received the second set of Ten

Commandments. At this same time, the Israelites were granted atonement for the sin of the Golden Calf. Jewish people have traditionally observed this holiday with a twenty-four hour period of fasting and intensive prayer. Most of the holiday is spent praying in the synagogue. God mandates that anyone who does not observe the regulations on this day must be cut off from his people. This event is celebrated on the 10th day of Tishri (usually in September or October).

Prophecy: The Day of Atonement is a prophecy of future redemption through the death and resurrection of Jesus Christ. There will be a redemption of Israel and a redemption of creation.

End-times: On the Day of Atonement, following the Ten Days of Awe, the High Priest enters the Holy of Holies to make atonement for everyone. In the end times, Jesus returns as our High Priest and makes eternal atonement for us.

Feast of Tabernacles

The Feast of Tabernacles (Feast of Ingathering or Sukkot) is a commemoration of the Israelite history. This festival lasts for seven days, with the first and eighth days being days of rest. As prescribed in the Bible, all native-born Israelites were to live in booths so the descendants would know that God had the Israelites live in tents when He brought them out of Egypt. Today, the religious Jewish people live in a Sukkah (or tabernacle) to honor the time when Israel lived in tents during their forty years in the desert.

The Feast of Tabernacles is a drastic transition from one of the most solemn holidays in the Jewish year (Yom Kippur, or the Day of Atonement) to one of the most joyous. The

Relaying the Word

festival is so joyful that it is commonly referred to as the season of rejoicing.

During earlier times, the high point of the celebration was the "drawing of water" ceremony when the people called upon the Lord to provide heavenly waters for their next harvest season. A grand event that was full of much pomp and drama, it reached its peak on the last day of Sukkot, at which time the priests filled a golden pitcher with water from the pool of Siloam and returned to the temple.

This feast is celebrated on the 15th to 22nd days of Tishri (usually in September or October).

Prophecy: The Feast of Tabernacles is a prophecy of God dwelling eternally with man. It points to a future Sukkot. On the last day of the feast, at the time of the drawing of water ceremony, Jesus stood and said, "If anyone is thirsty, let him come to me and drink. Whoever believes in me, will have streams of living water flowing from within him" (see John 7:37-38). Jesus was describing a time when all provisions will be made.

End-times: Feast of Tabernacles is a celebration commemorating the dwelling with God. It is synonymous with the thousand-year reign of Christ. Both are pictures of man living with God in a temporary dwelling.

Purim

Purim is a Jewish holiday that commemorates the saving of the Jewish people from Haman, who was planning to kill all the Jews as described in the book of Esther. It is observed on the 14th day of Adar (usually in March).

When Haman's name is read out loud during the public chanting of the book of Esther in the synagogue, the congregation makes noise to blot out his name, which occurs 54 times. On Purim, some people eat triangular pastries called *Hamantaschen* ("Haman's pockets") or *Oznei Haman* ("Haman's ears").

Recipe for Hamantaschen Cookies

3 beaten eggs
1 cup sugar
¾ cup vegetable oil
2 ½ teaspoons vanilla extract
½ cup orange juice
5 ½ cups all-purpose flour
1 tablespoon baking powder
12 oz. can of fruit pie filling (i.e. cherry, apple, blueberry)

In a large bowl, combine the eggs and sugar and stir until light and fluffy. Stir in the oil, vanilla, and juice. Stir in the flour and baking powder to form a stiff dough.

Roll out dough on a lightly floured surface to a thickness of about ¼ inch. Cut circles approximately 2 ½ inches in diameter. Place circles on a greased cookie sheet or baking stone. Pinch the edges of the circle to make three corners forming a "dish" in the shape of a triangle. Spoon 1 to 2 teaspoons of pie filling into the center of the triangles.

Bake in a 350°F preheated oven for 12 to 15 minutes.

Jerusalem Day

Jerusalem Day is an Israeli national holiday celebrating the reunification of Jerusalem and the establishment of Israeli control over the Old City after the 1967 Six-Day War. The holiday is observed on the 28th of Lyar (mid to late May).

Relaying the Word

Israel Independence Day

On May 14, 1948, the nation of Israel, which had not been an official state for about 2,000 years, was reborn in a day. It is celebrated on the 5th day of Lyar (around early May).

Hanukkah

In Hebrew, the word *hanukkah* means "dedication." This holiday commemorates the re-dedication of the holy Temple in Jerusalem in 165 B.C.E.

When the Jewish people regained control of the temple, they found that it had been spiritually defiled by the worship of foreign gods and the sacrificing of swine. To purify the Temple, they needed to burn ritual oil in the Temple's menorah for eight days; however, they had only one day's worth of oil. They lit the menorah anyway and by a miracle, the small amount of oil lasted the entire eight days. For this reason, Hanukkah is celebrated for eight days and nights. It starts on the 25th of the Jewish month of Kislev (late November-late December).

Hanukkah gelt refers to money as well as chocolate coins given to Jewish children on the festival of Hanukkah. Parents often give children chocolate gelt to use for the game played with a dreidel.

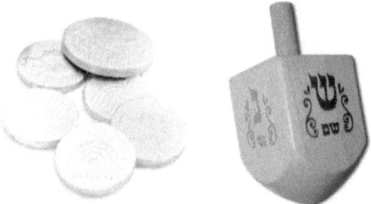

A dreidel is a four-sided spinning top, used in a game played during Hanukkah. Each side of the dreidel bears a letter of the Hebrew alphabet: נ (Nun), ג (Gimel), ה (Hei), ש (Shin), which together form the acronym for that when translated means a great miracle happened there.

Each player begins with an equal number (~10 to 15) of gelt or some other object. At the beginning of each round, every player puts one piece into the center pot. Each player then spins the dreidel once upon their turn. The letters on the dreidel also form a mnemonic for the rules of the game:

Nun (נ) means the player does nothing.
Hei (ה) means the player gets half of the pot.
Gimel (ג) means the player gets everything in the pot.
Shin (ש) means the player adds a piece to the pot.

8. Kings and Prophets of Judah and Israel

The Kingdom United

Years (BC)	King	Start / End	Prophet	Scripture
1050 - 1010	Saul	Good / Evil	Samuel	1 Sa 8-31 1 Ch 9-10
1010 - 970	David (Captain)	Good / Good	Samuel Nathan	1 Sa 16-31 2 Sa 1-24 1 Ki 1-2 1 Ch 11-29
970 - 930	Solomon (Son)	Good / Evil	Nathan	1 Ki 1-11 2 Ch 1-9

Illustration created by ©craigtowens.com and used with permission.

Craig T. Owens is the pastor of Calvary Assembly of God in Cedar Springs, Michigan (cscalvary.com) and an active blogger. Visit his website (craigtowens.com) for blog posts, book reviews, and other information.

Relaying the Word
The Kingdom Divided

Judah					Israel				
Years	King	Start / End	Prophet	Scripture	Years	King	Start / End	Prophet	Scripture
931 - 913	Rehoboam (Son)	Evil / Evil		1 Ki 12, 14 2 Ch 10-12	931 - 910	Jeroboam I (servant)	Evil / Evil	Abijah	1 Ki 12-14 2 Ch 10
913 - 911	Abijah (Son)	Evil / Evil	Shemaiah	1 Ki 15 2 Ch 13					
					910 - 909	Nadab (son)	Evil / Evil		1 Ki 15
					909 - 886	Baasha	Evil / Evil	Jehu	1 Ki 16
911 - 870	Asa (Son)	Good/Good	Hanani	1 Ki 15 2 Ch 14-16	886 - 885	Elah (Son)	Evil / Evil		1 Ki 16
					885	Zimri (Captain)	Evil / Evil	Micaiah	1 Ki 16
					885 - 874	Omri (Captain)	Evil / Evil	Elijah 1 Ki 17-19 1 Ki 21 2 Ki 1-2	1 Ki 16
					874 - 853	Ahab (Son)	Evil / Evil		1 Ki 17 2 Ch 18
870 - 848	Jehoshaphat (Son)	Good/Good		1 Ki 22 2 Ch 17-20	853 - 852	Ahaziah (Son)	Evil / Evil		1 Ki 22 2 Ki 1
848 - 841	Jehoram (Son)	Evil / Evil		2 Ki 8 2 Ch 21	852 - 841	Joram (Son of Ahab)	Evil / Evil	Elisha 1 Ki 19 2 Ki 2-9 2 Ki 13	2 Ki 3
841	Ahaziah (Son)	Evil / Evil		2 Ki 8-9 2 Ch 22					
841 - 835	Athaliah (mother)	Evil / Evil		2 Ki 11 2 Ch 22-23	841 - 814	Jehu (Captain)	Good / Evil		2 Ki 9-10
835 - 796	Joash (son of Ahaziah)	Good / Evil	Joel	2 Ki 11-12 2 Ch 23-24	814 - 798	Jehoahaz (Son)	Evil / Evil		2 Ki 13
796 - 767	Amaziah (son)	Good / Evil		2 Ki 14 2 Ch 25	798 - 782	Jehoash (Son)	Evil / Evil		2 Ki 13-14
					782 - 753	Jeroboam II (Son)	Evil / Evil		2 Ki 14
767 - 740	Uzziah aka Azariah (Son)	Good/Evil		2 Ki 15 2 Ch 26	753 - 752	Zechariah (Son)	Evil / Evil	Amos Hosea Jonah (in Nineveh)	2 Ki 15
					752	Shallum	Evil / Evil		2 Ki 15
					752 - 742	Menahem	Evil / Evil		2 Ki 15
					742 - 740	Pekahiah (Son)	Evil / Evil		2 Ki 15
748 - 732	Jotham (Son)	Good/Good	Isaiah Micah	2 Ki 15 2 Ch 27	752 - 740 (rival) 733 - 722 (solo)	Pekah (Captain)	Evil / Evil		2 Ki 15
732 - 716	Ahaz (Son)	Evil / Evil		2 Ki 16 2 Ch 28 Is 7	732 - 722	Hoshea	Evil / Evil		2 Ki 17
716 - 687	Hezekiah (Son)	Good/Good		2 Ki 18-20 2 Ch 29-32 Is 36-39	Israel into Assyrian captivity - 722 BC				
687 - 642	Manasseh (Son)	Evil / Good		2 Ki 21 2 Ch 33				Nahum	
642 - 640	Amon (Son)	Evil / Evil		2 Ki 21 2 Ch 33					
640 - 608	Josiah (Son)	Good/Good		2 Ki 22-23 2 Ch 34-35					
608	Jehoahaz (Son)	Evil / Evil		2 Ki 23 2 Ch 36					
608 - 597	Jehoiakim (Son of Josiah)	Evil / Evil	Habakkuk Zephaniah Jeremiah	2 Ki 23-24 2 Ch 36				Daniel	
597	Jehoiachin (Son)	Evil / Evil	Ezekiel (Lamentations)	2 Ki 24-25 2 Ch 36					
597 - 586	Zedekiah (Son of Josiah)	Evil / Evil		2 Ki 24-25 2 Ch 36				Obadiah	
Judah into Babylonian captivity - 586 BC									

Illustration created by ©craigtowens.com and used with permission.

Craig T. Owens is the pastor of Calvary Assembly of God in Cedar Springs, Michigan (cscalvary.com), and an active blogger. Visit his website (craigtowens.com) for blog posts, book reviews, and other information.

9. Revelation Helps

In general, the book is divided into sevens: seven letters to the churches, seven seals, seven trumpets, and seven bowls.

The seven letters warn the churches of the end times. In the end-time events, the seven seals are followed by the seven trumpets, which in turn are followed by the seven bowls of wrath.

Seven Seals

The scroll that originates from the throne of God *in heaven* has seven seals that are opened *in heaven* by Jesus Christ; however, most of the events (except the fifth seal) happen *on earth*. The seven seals are not a part of the contents of the scroll, but in fact are conditions to its opening. Furthermore, the opening of a seal is not contingent upon completing what was designated by a previous seal. In other words, the opening of the third seal does not depend upon the completion of the events in the second seal.

The first four of the seven seals are commonly referred to as the Four Horsemen or the Four Horses of the Apocalypse. These four horses are not unique to the book of Revelation. Zechariah, who saw four horses of the same color, was told that they represented the four spirits of heaven that stand in the presence of the Lord of the whole world. He saw the black horse go north, the white horse go west, the pale horse go south, and the red horse (by inference) go east. These spirits (often thought of as senior angels) go throughout the earth at God's command to accomplish His will.

Seven Trumpets

After the opening of the seventh seal, there will be silence in heaven for half an hour as a solemn reverence of the opening of the seven seals and the yet-to-come blowing of the seven trumpets.

The seven trumpets, which resemble the plagues upon Egypt, will be sent to warn mankind and to call mankind to repentance. They are designed to arrest the attention of the world so that everyone can hear the Gospel. In addition, the trumpets will create an environment that will sober every living person to the point at which they will at least consider the Gospel. This proclamation of the Gospel will attract everyone sincere in heart, but will powerfully repel those who rebel against God. Thus, they also serve to further divide the people before the Great Harvest.

The Seven Bowls of God's Wrath

The seven bowls are actually seven paybacks for those who received the mark of the beast. Ultimately, the purpose of the seven last plagues is vengeance.

The seven plagues have been compared to God's warnings given in Leviticus:

* *If after all this you will not listen to Me, I will punish you for your sins *seven times over* (see Leviticus 26:18).
* *If you remain hostile toward Me and refuse to listen to Me, I will multiply your afflictions *seven times over*, as your sins deserve (see Leviticus 26:21).
* *If in spite of these things you do not accept My correction but continue to be hostile toward Me, I Myself will be hostile toward you and will afflict

Relaying the Word

you for your sins *seven times over* (see Leviticus 26:23–24).

*If in spite of this you still do not listen to Me but continue to be hostile toward Me, then in My anger I will be hostile toward you, and I Myself will punish you for your sins *seven times over* (see Leviticus 26:27–28).

Unlike the trumpets, the bowls are not warnings; they are God's long-suffering wrath. They will follow a similar pattern as the seven trumpets: four affecting creation (earth, sea, water, cosmos); two associated with the beast or man; and the final one directed toward the nations. The seventh bowl will directly follow the sixth bowl. There will be no interlude, as with the six and seventh seals and trumpets. These pauses will provide a time for witnessing and reflecting upon the Gospel. During the pouring out of the bowls of wrath, the time for repentance will be long past.

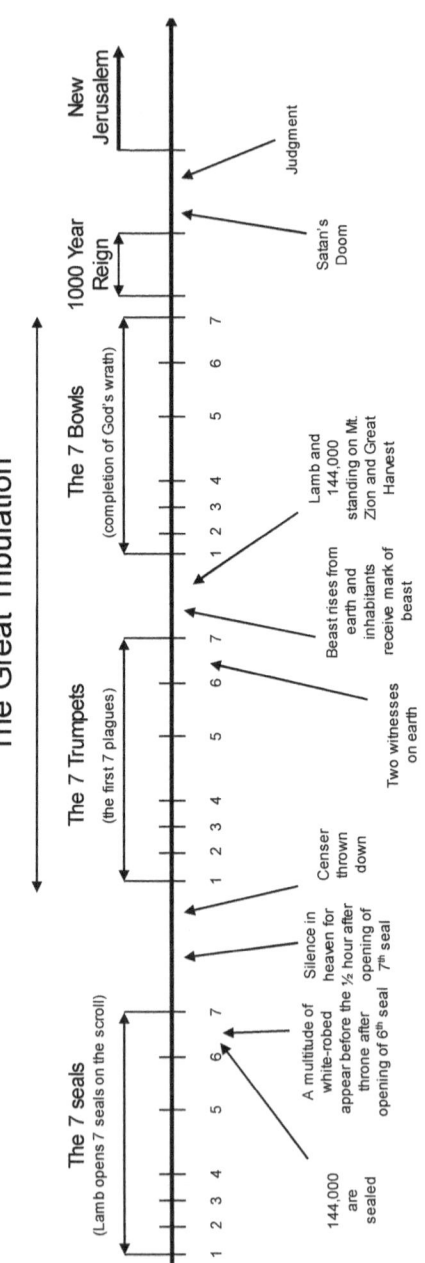

The Short Version of John's Revelation

*The first six seals are opened, but the consequences of the first four are held back until the sealing of the 144,000 Jews on earth and the rapture of the redeemed.

*After the sixth seal and before the seventh, the 144,000 are sealed and the redeemed are raptured.

*The seventh seal is broken, and there is silence in heaven for half an hour. Then, the angel throws to earth the censer filled with fire from the altar, and the seven trumpets (a warning and a call to repentance) begin.

*First six trumpets blow and the consequences occur.

*After sixth trumpet, the 144,000 Jews are joined with Christ on Mount Zion, and then there is a Great Harvest of those people who turned to God and didn't take the mark of the beast. At this point, there are no more believers on earth.

*The seventh trumpet proclaims the kingdom of God and is followed by the seven bowls of God's wrath.

*The seven bowls of wrath are poured out on the people who refused to accept God and who worshiped the beast instead. These bowls contain God's vengeance on these people.

*After the wrath is finished, Babylon is destroyed and the beast and his army are cast into hell while Jesus reigns for 1,000 years.

*At the end of the 1,000 years, the beast is released for one last chance at repentance. Instead, he mounts an attack against God and His people. The beast is bound, and he and his army are cast into hell for eternity.

*God judges *all* people at the Great White Throne of Judgment.

*God restores the earth and brings down the New Jerusalem, where the redeemed will live with Him forever.

Relaying the Word

Review Request

I hope this book helped you to start a *Relaying the Word* Bible study and has inspired you to live more fully in the Word.

Now that you've read this book, please let other folks know about *Relaying the Word*. Let's share the knowledge and help people to get involved in community Bible study.

About the Author

BEYR REYES received her doctorate degree in biomedical science. She has produced over 200 publications in science, medicine, and Christian genres. In addition, she has worked in the drug industry since 2005 as a regulatory writer for major international pharmaceutical and biotech companies. (Beyr Reyes is Jennifer Minigh's pen name for the Christian genre.)

You can contact Beyr Reyes via email, Twitter, or Facebook:

Beyr.Reyes@ShadeTreePublishing.com

@JenniferMinigh

Facebook.com/Jennifer.Minigh

Other Books by Beyr Reyes

The Big Picture
2011 Readers' Favorite Bronze Award

Most folks know the stories about Creation, the Jewish nation, and Jesus, but they don't know how all these things are connected. This book provides a broad perspective of the Bible that will help the beginner place events and their purposes together. For the readers who always have their heads buried in certain passages, this book is a refreshing step back to help illuminate the big picture.

Subject Your Flesh
2014 CSPA e-Book of the Year

Need to get control of your life? Tired of constant dieting? Fed up with bad habits? Subjection is the answer that lasts. Learn how to eradicate the problem areas in your life. Take control of your flesh and turn your life around using the Word of God.

Relaying the Word

Fast Answers:
When You Need Answers Now

Other fasting books tell you why to fast or explain the importance thereof, but leave you guessing how to even start. This book puts legs on your intentions so that you can walk it out. *Fast Answers* has mapped out fasting plans with a clear starting point, destination, and goal. The plans come in one-, three-, or seven-day varieties and are tailored to specific prayer needs. No longer will you fumble your way through a fast. With this book, you will find your way to the answers you need right now. This book isn't about fast answers (as in quick ones). It's about fast answers (as in seeking-God ones).

Make a Choice
2011 Readers' Favorite Silver Award

This book is a continuum of revelation designed to challenge your foundational beliefs and then challenge you to stand on those beliefs. In Unit 1 (Choose Your Beliefs), you will ask yourself questions like: Is God really God? Is Jesus God? Is the Bible true? In Unit 2 (Live Like You Mean It), you will ask yourself: Am I really a Christian? Am I really saved? Am I really forgiven? All along the way, you will make decisions that will affect your life forever.

Relaying the Word

Renewable Energy: a short story about second chances

The stories of the Bible from an alien perspective, *Renewable Energy* explores the purpose of life and how to get a second chance at it while being caught in the middle of a great battle for "soular" energy.

489: a short story about forgiveness
2016 CSPA General Fiction Book of the Year

Loaded with plot twists and surprises, this short story delivers a powerful message about forgiveness and how our lives affect other people, even those we don't know. Widely endorsed by therapists, this book helps readers to be set free from the bondage of unforgiveness.

Relaying the Word

**Your Write Calling:
Is Writing Right for You?**

Have you been toying with the idea of becoming a writer? If so, this book is for you. Learn what it means, and what it takes, to be a Christian writer. After reading this book, you will understand what the call to write looks like. In addition, you will know how to get equipped and what to write. Endorsed by Jerry B. Jenkins, this book contains soul-searching questions to help you decide on your calling all along the way.

Relaying the Word

Relaying the Word
NOTES

Relaying the Word

www.ingramcontent.com/pod-product-compliance
Lightning Source LLC
Chambersburg PA
CBHW021443080526
44588CB00009B/664